CALLIGRAPHY IN THE GRAPHIC ARTS

The professional designer of printed material is able to call upon a vast range of typographic letter styles to give visual expression to a message, b   n education has neglected calligraphy for twenty-five y   ing many designers with no knowledge or experience   ft whose forms lie behind e   tter, and little   of its graphic potential.

Callig   fro   a few s   design t   og o ypes a   er pieces   e   y's display ypes are not suitable – but has recently come gloriously alive again, mostly through the work of enthusiastic amateurs, especially in America.

The purpose of this book is to re-connect design and calligraphy. Its concise text and clear illustrations will be of particular interest to designers and students. Starting with typographic letters familiar to designers the author uses the pen to reconstruct and develop them creatively, then shows a variety of techniques including re-touching, paste-up, stencilling, the use of resists and masks, photocopiers and unconventional tools and writing surfaces. Many examples of calligraphically derived designs are shown, the principles of using calligraphy with type and its placing within typographic formats are discussed, and experimental pen and brush scripts conclude the book.

Calligraphy in the Graphic Arts will also help calligraphers who wish to adapt their skills to the requirements of print and technology, and art directors who want to use calligraphic lettering in publicity or editorial design. This is the final book of three that the author has produced covering contemporary letter-making arts, and because it deals with written letters it underpins the other two, *Creative Lettering: Drawing and Design* and *Carving Letters in Stone and Wood*.

Michael Harvey is an internationally known lettering designer and teacher, with great experience in the fields of bookjacket, logotype, type design and stone-cut lettering.

MICHAEL HARVEY

Calligraphy

IN THE GRAPHIC ARTS

INTRODUCTION BY HERMANN ZAPF

THE BODLEY HEAD · *LONDON*

A CIP catalogue record for this book
is available from the British Library.

ISBN 0-370-31139-6

© Michael Harvey 1988
Printed in Great Britain for
The Bodley Head Ltd,
32 Bedford Square, London WC1B 3EL
by Butler & Tanner Ltd, Frome and London
First published in 1988

CONTENTS

Introduction by Hermann Zapf

After the Second World War a strong Bauhaus influence prevailed in many Western countries. Designers preferred sanserif letters and several typefaces in this style were designed and widely used. In these years some art directors thought calligraphy too personal, too expressionistic and emotional. Today those same people have discovered in calligraphy a desirable individuality and human touch, often preferring it to the neutral forms of sanserif alphabets. But many letterforms which are classified as calligraphy are poor and amateurish, and some modern calligraphers do more harm to art and design standards than the old sanserif dogmatists. Unfortunately, the problem is that mediocre work is too often shown to clients. Art directors should be more selective when commissioning calligraphy and this may be the reason why calligraphy sometimes has such a negative image in the graphic design world.

But take a look at Michael Harvey's examples in this book, see how he interprets letterforms using different tools to transfer letters into real calligraphy. Each detail is convincing. This is the way in which calligraphy will conquer the graphic arts and build up the reputation which this art should also have within the wider sphere of commercial art.

With his three earlier publications *Lettering Design* (1975), *Creative Lettering: Drawing and Design* (1985) and *Carving Letters in Stone and Wood* (1987), Michael Harvey's standard books now cover all areas of the use of letterforms. They form a complete compendium of creative graphic design, based on years of experience and his training in the Edward Johnston tradition that respects legibility, guided by discipline and skill, as the first service to the reader.

In his books you will find no dry routine instructions, but friendly help in developing the reader's self-confidence in his daily professional work. Michael Harvey gives advice on the making of many eye-catching and effective designs. These four volumes give guidelines for beginners and inspiration for the professional designer, helping to raise calligraphy into a contemporary art form.

Good letterforms in a variety of styles and expressions are needed to serve the wide-ranging graphic community. We have new tools and materials at hand today which we should use in our daily work. The quill still has its uses but we should take advantage of fibre-tipped pens, as recommended in this book. The broad-edged pen – once the only accepted and classic tool of calligraphers – is now only one of the modern alternatives which are available.

The whole condition in which we work, the environment around us, has changed completely since electronics squeezed themselves into designers' studios. Calligraphy will have more influence on graphic design in the future than in the past decades, especially in a world dominated by computer graphics. Although it is possible to perform all kinds of video tricks on a personal computer, the specific expressive quality of hand-written letterforms can never be imitated precisely on a video screen. The hand will always have its own distinctive and lively expression, so to train the hand and broaden our skill is a way to compete with the many electronic facilities around us, not only to defend artistic creativity in the future but also to keep control of the new technologies.

Edward Johnston's outstanding book *Writing and Illuminating and Lettering* (1906) was the guide for the restoration of calligraphy after the turn of this century, and is a great guide for all of us. Let us hope that Michael Harvey's books may provide the graphic arts with the additional up-to-date developments of the great heritage of calligraphy that will enable it to survive creatively in the modern world of electronics.

Author's preface

Five hundred years ago, when the manuscript book was central to our culture, calligraphy was *the* graphic art, but the advent of the printed book removed the broad-edged pen from its essential role as a letter-making (and designing) instrument, and now the written letter is only one of the elements that may be employed in a graphic designer's repertoire. That calligraphy – a fairly recent . term – survives today is largely due to the revival, mostly amateur, that began in England when Edward Johnston's classes at the Central School of Arts and Crafts in London in the early years of this century attracted many enthusiastic students. This revival has recently gathered strength from America, where calligraphic societies abound, and from the many books now available to meet the requirements of this movement, still largely amateur, which produces work of sometimes dazzling originality while basing itself on the apparently out-of-date technology of pen, ink and paper.

While this revival continues to flourish, occasionally crossing into the area of fine art, the graphic arts in the shape of a highly competitive, print-based and computer-assisted technology in which the photographic image is paramount, rely almost entirely on typeforms generated by photography or laser beam. Manufacturers of photo-composing systems and transfer lettering compete energetically in bringing out new ranges of alphabets in many styles and weights, often grotesquely distorted revivals of ugly and/or illegible letter-forms. There are even types that more or less successfully imitate the written letter (the first typeface, made by Gutenburg in the fifteenth century, was an imitation of one of the current blackletter scripts) but a typographic system will never be able to rival the flexibility of writing. Technology notwithstanding, the handwritten letter has retained a humble place in advertising and publicity material, notably in brush scripts – the most difficult style for type to render – whose freely handled forms were popular for many years, keeping several highly skilful artists employed until the arrival of dry transfer lettering in the 'sixties effectively killed off this minor artform. Recent signs indicate that a revival is underway, while a few lucky individuals, amongst whom I count myself, have continued to make a living as lettering designers.

This, then, is the situation today. On the one hand a mostly amateur but sometimes highly creative movement that values its freedom from technology and takes pride in individual work, and on the other the professional, highly technical, deadline-meeting and cost-conscious world of the graphic arts where designers and art directors perhaps view with disdain the, to them, purveyors of what John Brinkley dismissed as 'calligraphic knitting'. This conflict between craft and design is reflected in art colleges where, as design courses strive to become ever more professional, calligraphy has virtually disappeared from the curriculum. The purpose of this book is to break down the barriers and bring these two worlds closer together for the benefit of each. To do this I have based myself firmly in the camp of the professionals by taking the typographic letters with which they are familiar, using calligraphy to explain their forms and to develop variations leading on to further creative possibilities.

This approach may not appeal to traditional calligraphers but I believe its value lies in its contemporary relevance. Using typefaces (which of course derive from a calligraphic past) as a basis has the virtue of making the reader I envisage, namely the practising graphic designer or student, feel at home in a way that presenting, say, yet another example of a tenth-century bookhand would not. Following this policy I have as far as possible recommended the use of the kinds of instruments designers are familiar with, especially the fibre-tipped pen, instead of the more usual steel-nibbed pens fitted with reservoirs and requiring special ink. If the reader is inspired to study calligraphy in greater depth then the world of quills, vellum and gold leaf may be a powerful attraction. Here, though, it might be a deterrent.

Calligraphy in the Graphic Arts will also be useful to those calligraphers who want to adapt their skills to the requirements of print and technology, and help art directors who wish to commission calligraphic lettering appreciate the exciting (and subtle) choices available. This is the final book of three devoted to what I call 'a trinity of letter-making arts' and, because it deals with written letters, it is fundamental to the other two, *Creative Lettering: Drawing and Design* and *Carving Letters in Stone and Wood*. These books are an attempt to provide much essential and relevant information, advice and inspiration for those wishing to write, draw or carve letters: three distinct but interdependent arts all worth our serious attention.

For permission to reproduce designs the author wishes to thank the following: Lyn Gathercole; The Thimble Press; English National Opera, and the estate of George Bernard Shaw for the quotation on page 29.

As explained in the Author's preface, the policy of this book is to avoid the use of special calligraphic tools, where this is possible, and to work with the pens and brushes that are a part of a designer's regular equipment. Most of the examples in these pages were made with fibre-tipped pens and re-touched.

Pens   It is a good idea to make a collection of fibre-tipped pens, both pointed and broad-edged, in varying thicknesses and widths. Try to obtain pens marked 'permanent' because these will allow re-touching with white watercolour. It will be found that some pens work best after they have been in use for a while, so try to break in a new pen on some other work before using it for writing, and remember that a pen that is near exhaustion will produce letters with an interesting texture. A fibre-tipped pen that combines a fine point with considerable flexibility is the Mars Graphic 3000. In use it is similar to a brush, responding to pressure changes when writing. A range of cartridge pens called Artpen includes three styles of nib – broad-edged in five line thicknesses; round-ended in three sizes; pointed in two sizes – which work smoothly and have some of the flexibility that fibre-tipped pens lack. They will produce finer lines than most fibre-tipped pens and the round-ended versions are good for writing monoline letters. The only disadvantage of the Artpen is that the cartridge ink is not waterproof, making re-touching difficult. They are comparatively expensive.

Designers are usually equipped with technical pens and will find the finer sizes useful for refining the edges of letters as well as strengthening serifs and other details. For copperplate writing a pointed, very flexible nib is essential, either straight or cranked (as shown below) to facilitate writing.

Brushes   Round hair nylon brushes, which will make a fine point and spread under pressure, are suitable for writing brush scripts, and flat square-ended brushes called *brights* can be used in the same way as a broad-edged pen to make strokes of varying thickness. Experiment with different brushes, including fat round ones and the stiff varieties designed for stencil work. Keep one fine-pointed brush for re-touching and remember that an old, battered brush that is useless for painting may produce unexpectedly vigorous lettering. The very flexible and responsive Chinese brush shown below can be used for large-scale work, and if space permits a house-painter's brush

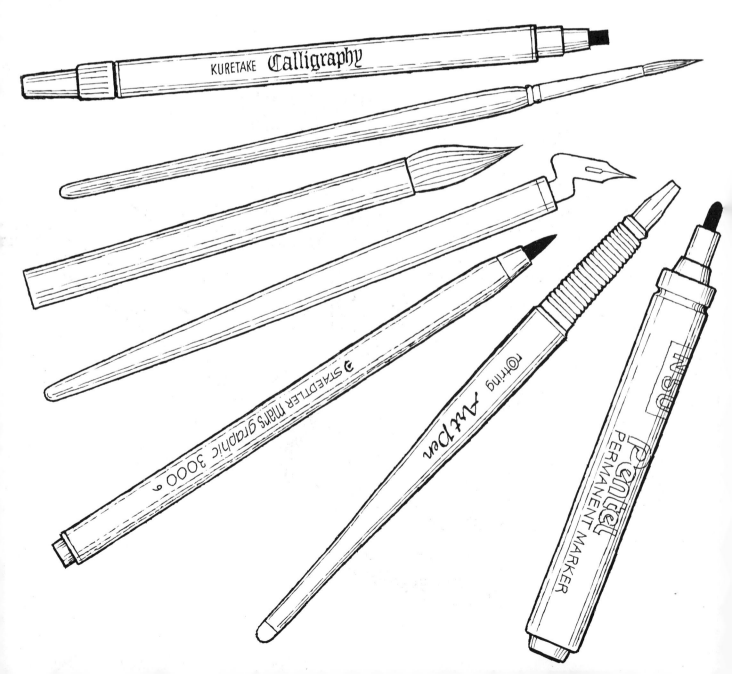

can be used, preferably on a vertical surface (such as a wall).

Paper   A fairly smooth surface, not too absorbent and with a slight roughness to help pen control is best for most calligraphic work. Detail or bond paper in pads is ideal, but be careful not to use a paper that causes the pen to bleed. The thicker drawing papers with rough surfaces will produce interesting textures in the writing, while very absorbent papers such as blotting paper can lead to unusual effects. Avoid all artboards (unless drawing the kind of lettering shown on page 35) because their smooth surfaces offer no resistance to the pen, allowing it to slide out of control.

Ink   Use black waterproof drawing ink for brush-writing and be sure to wash brushes thoroughly afterwards. With metal nibs a non-waterproof ink will produce finer lines.

Paint   White gouache for re-touching and black gouache for use as an alternative to ink for brushwork – its thicker consistency can be used to advantage in expressive writing, and, like ink, it can be thinned with water to make softly toned letters.

Glue   Rubber cement for paste-up work and as a resist medium.

Other equipment   Scissors and a craft knife (the knife will be useful for separating letters to make spacing adjustments); drafting tape; pencils (soft to medium-hard, for guide lines and preliminary sketching); an eraser to remove pencil work; crayons (their use as a resist is shown on page 45); paper towels for wiping brushes and pens, but also as an experimental writing surface (see page 44). As well as these sundry items – a list that could grow indefinitely – it is desirable to have a drawing board that can be adjusted to a comfortable writing angle, a comfortable chair and the usual drafting equipment such as a tee-square, set square (triangle) and ruler. A good light source is essential: avoid direct sunlight and use an adjustable lamp when daylight fails. Keep a large soft brush handy to clear the working surface of eraser debris and a waste-paper bin large enough to accept all the reject pieces of work.

The photocopier is a wonderful device, much used in the making of this book. Re-touching photocopies is sometimes difficult because watercolour does not readily adhere to the copier ink surface, but perseverance with two or three coats of thick paint will usually overcome the problem.

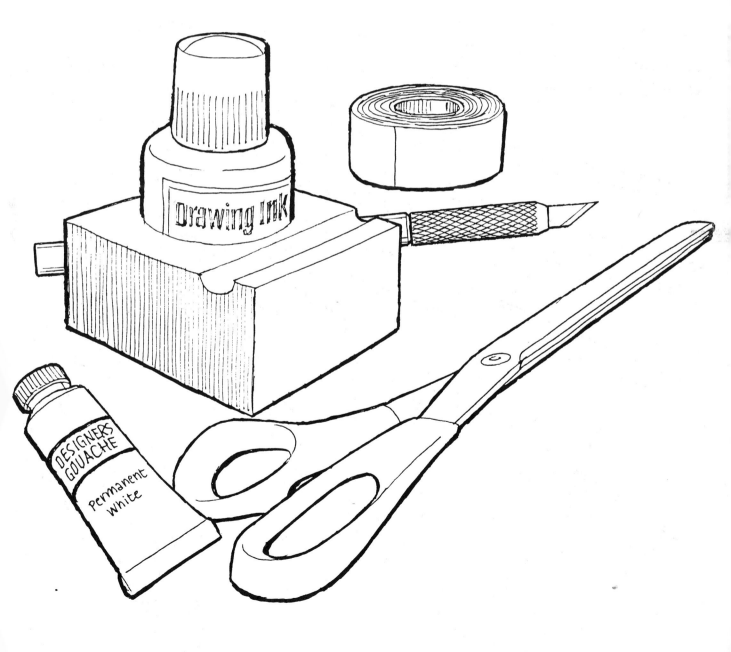

Broad-edged pen strokes

Whether cut from reeds or quills the broad-edged pen was the major letter-making tool until the invention of printing, its characteristic thick and thin strokes surviving in many typographic letters. A modern equivalent of these pens is the broad-edged fibre-tipped pen which is available in various widths, and this kind of pen is used in this demonstration and for the majority of the examples in this book.

Writing is best done on a sloping surface of about 10 degrees and when held as shown below the pen's angle to the writing surface will be approximately 60 degrees. It is best to find the position on the writing surface where the writing feels easiest (or least difficult) and to move the paper along as the writing progresses, keeping the hand in the same position throughout.

Because the writing arm is connected to a shoulder and does not grow directly out of the middle of the chest it is natural that the pen will be at an angle to the writing line, as shown in position (1) below. This tilt of the pen's edge – approximately 30 degrees – results in the typical vertical, horizontal, diagonal and curved strokes shown here. Notice that the widest stroke is the top left to bottom right

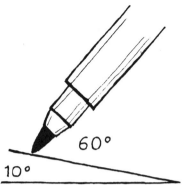

1

2

diagonal while the top right to bottom left diagonal and the horizontal are thinnest. The curves have a pronounced tilt or stress, swelling from thin to thick and back to thin. Several other strokes resulting from this pen angle are shown at (1a).

It is possible to ignore the natural angle described above and pull the pen round so that its edge is parallel to the writing line, as in (2), to produce a full width vertical, matching diagonals, a very thin horizontal and curves without any tilt. Other strokes are shown at (2a). This rather difficult to maintain

writing angle is rarely used but can be seen in some kinds of uncial letter (see page 20).

The very rare pen position shown at (3) is here mainly for demonstration purposes. In this case the opposite of position (2) occurs, with a very thin vertical, wide horizontal, matching half-width diagonals and curves weighted at top and bottom and thin at the sides. Other strokes resulting from this eccentric pen angle are shown at (3a). They are suggestive of some oriental scripts that employ a great variety of pen angles.

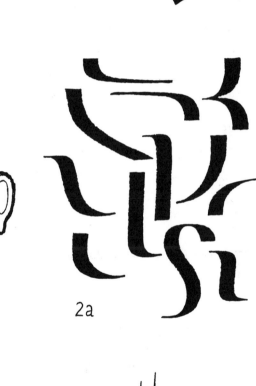

1a

2a

3

3a

Flexible pointed pen and brush strokes

The important difference between the writing tools described here and the broad-edged pen is that, whereas the edged pen produces thick and thin strokes that vary according to the angle and direction of movement, flexible pens and brushes require pressure to make thicker lines. Increasing pressure brings thicker lines as the nib opens or the brush's bristles spread to release a wider flow of ink. The illustration below (1) shows this happening with a steel nib and above some typical vertical, horizontal, diagonal and curved strokes.

A recently introduced pointed instrument which has the feel of a brush with some of a pen's rigidity is the Mars Graphic 3000 pen. If this is held vertically above the writing sur-

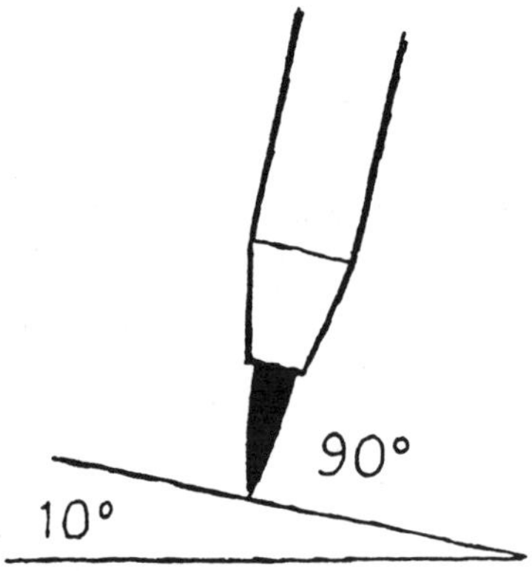

90°

10°

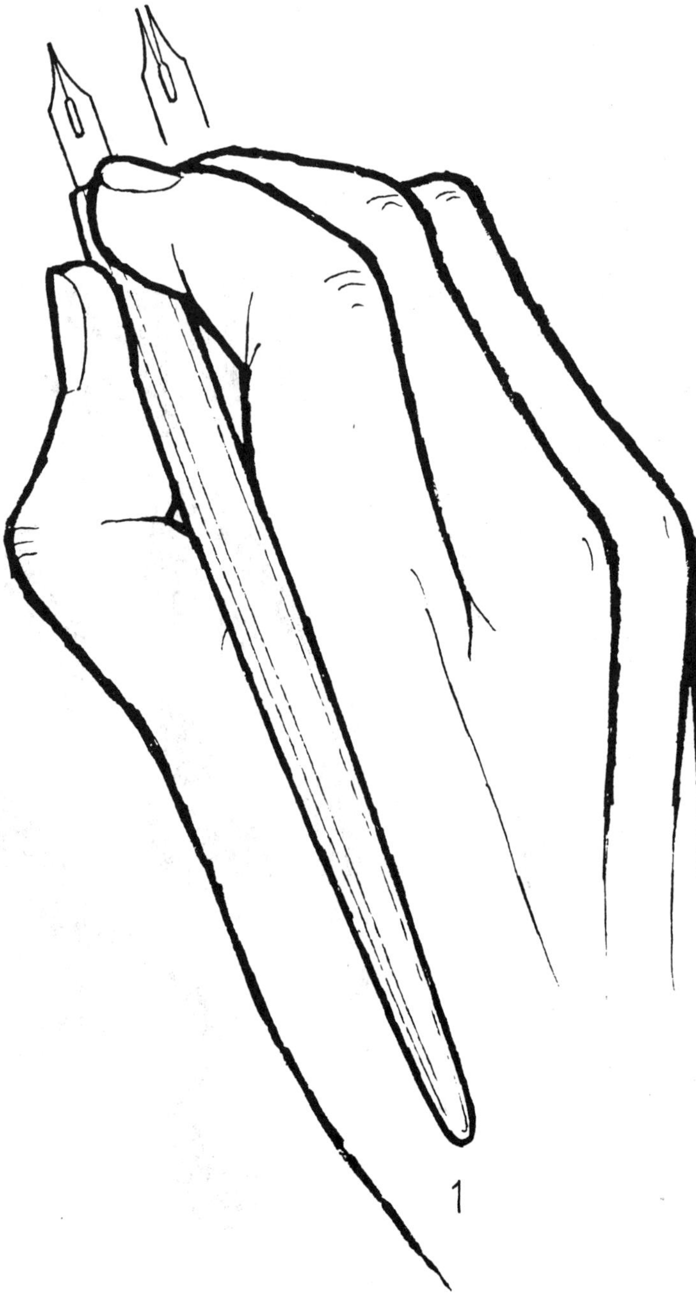

1

2

face, as shown left and at (2) below, the marks it makes will be similar to those of a pointed pen but requiring less pressure. Further examples of both tools' stroke-making are shown at (1a) and (2a). Typical pointed pen scripts are the copperplate styles described on page 32.

Pointed brushes respond to changes in writing pressure to a far greater degree than the steel nib. Both pressure and angle can be altered so that even quite a thin brush produces very wide strokes as its bristles are worked on their side. The variety of marks that a brush can make are infinite – a few are shown at (3a) – and many brush scripts have been developed for their flavour of informality and as a contrast to the more rigid typographic letter.

1a

2a

3

3a

The geometric basis of capital letters is well demonstrated in Paul Renner's Futura, shown right, and in the diagram below. This sanserif, monoline letter uses classic roman proportions – some letters wide, some narrow – and is a good model for writing practice with a pointed fibre-tipped pen. The stroke-making sequence is shown in the alphabet below, with alternative forms for some characters. Although it may seem easier to make letters *C, O* and *S* in one stroke the sequence shown will give more control over their forms.

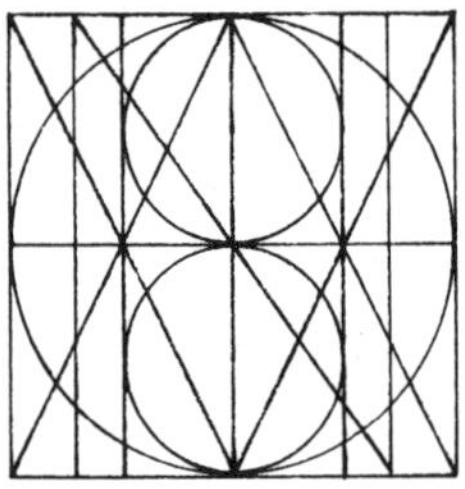

ABCDEFGHIJK
LMNOPQRST
UVWXYZ

Typeface: Futura

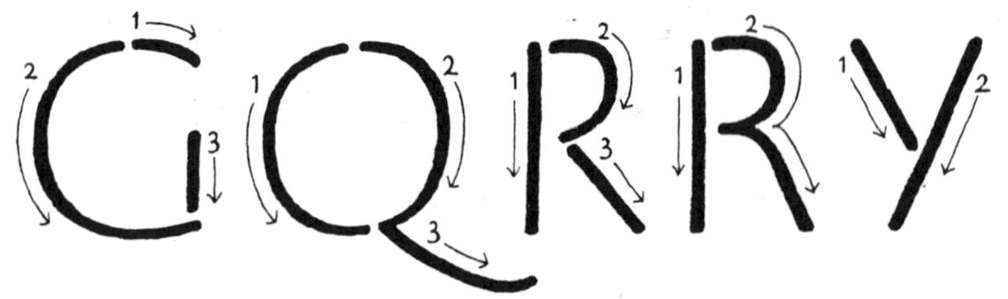

A B C D E F G H I J
K L M N O P Q R
S T U V W X Y Z
G Q Q R R Y

Use fine fibre-tipped pens or Rotring technical pens to make smaller letters, simplifying the stroke-making sequence to suit the small scale where this seems necessary. This will develop skill in type indication on layouts and visuals and although not writing as generally understood it will instil a habit of consistent stroke-making that is essential in calligraphy.

DESIGNER
BOOKJACKET CHAPTER HEADING
LETTER SPACING TYPOGRAPHIC SPECIFICATION

A A A A A A A A A A A A A A A A A A

Even when using such plain letters as these capitals some variety in line thickness and expressive quality can be achieved by using different pens and papers. Use pointed rather than broad-edged pens and notice that where the ink bleeds into an absorbent paper an attractive, rough-edged line may result. The group of letters shown left vary both in size and line quality. For more about papers see page 44.

The rendering of the groups of words below shows the changes in weight achieved by writing with pens of an increasing thickness, while compressing the letter proportions produces yet another variation.

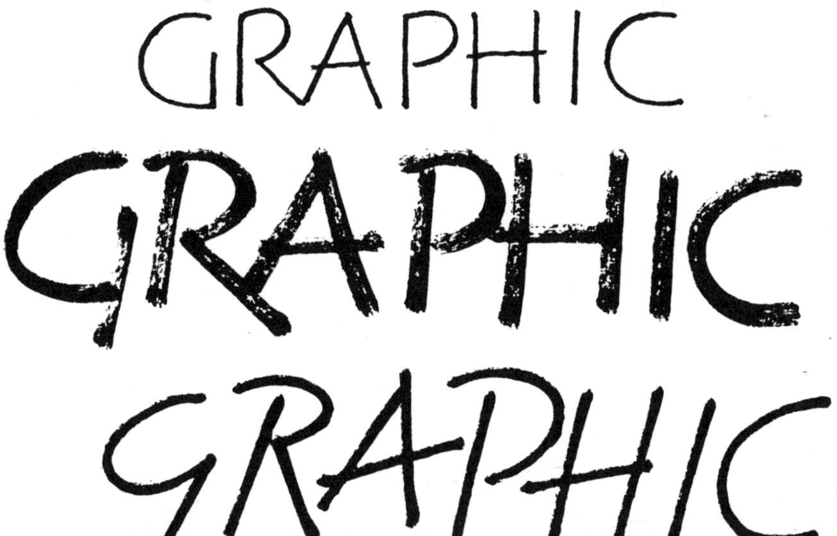

THE
OTHER
SIDE
OF
THE
TRACK

THE
OTHER
SIDE
OF
THE
TRACK

**THE
OTHER
SIDE
OF
THE
TRACK**

THE OTHER SIDE OF THE TRACK

GRAPHIC

GRAPHIC

GRAPHIC

The American calligrapher Lloyd Reynolds observed that in lettering the eye is conservative, wanting to recognise the forms with which it is familiar, while the hand is innovative, impatient of formality, and tries to take short cuts as it guides the pen. This tension between eye and hand is evident as the writing speed increases. Letters begin to lose their separateness, to join and to incline in the direction of the writing, the lively cursive quality that results being achieved at the expense of the original forms. Writing speed has been one of the influences through which letterforms evolved up until the time of the invention of printing types. Once familiar with these simple capitals it is enjoyable to practise writing them with increasing freedom, as shown left.

The usual variations in stroke width in roman capitals are clearly shown in Hermann Zapf's elegant typeface Optima, whose proportions are similar to Futura. The written forms that underlie this letter can be reconstructed with a broad-edged pen approximately one-tenth the height of the letter held at a shallow angle, following the sequence shown in the alphabet below. To achieve the thin verticals in *M* and *N* the broad edge should be twisted to 60 degrees. It will be seen that the strokes produced lack the slight waisting of the typographic letters, a subtle effect that can be obtained by pressure variations when writing with steel nibs or quill pens, or with the rigid fibre-tipped pen by twisting its broad edge from 0 to 30 degrees and back to 0 degrees as it travels down a vertical stem, as shown in detail (c) below.

Optima lacks the usual serifs of roman capitals and four ways of adding serifs to these written letters are shown in the enlarged details below. Detail (a)

ABCDEFGHIJK
LMNOPQRST
UVWXYZ

Typeface: Optima

is the simplest kind of serif, a rounded lead-in stroke to the left of the vertical and a lead-out stroke to the right. An alternative serif made by the pen travelling horizontally before moving down the vertical is also shown. Detail (b) shows another simple serif made by a horizontal pen stroke ending vertical stems. At endings to horizontal strokes a slight twisting of the pen to a steeper angle will give a thickening at the end with a short hairline to finish, or the pen may be turned onto one corner and pulled down to produce a curved hairline. Detail (c) shows the pen manipulation already described above, with the changes in angle producing curved serifs as the broad edge is

twisted into a vertical position at the end of horizontal strokes, and vertical strokes being completed with horizontal hairlines made by the pen on its thinnest edge. Detail (d) shows the serif achieved by the broad edge held horizontally and pulled down in a curve into the vertical and leaving in another curve on the baseline, returning to complete the horizontals and add an extra balancing curve at both ends to overlap and blend with the vertical. When used in conjunction with the waisted strokes shown in (c) this method produces the most sophisticated letterforms, but these techniques require great skill. In type design these qualities are achieved by drawing

rather than writing the letters, giving the designer absolute control over their forms.

The choice of ratio between width of pen and height of letter is quite wide, and the extremes of lightness and boldness that can be obtained by varying the stroke width for letters of the same height is shown right. As thickness of stroke increases some proportions alter to accommodate the extra weight and blackness.

IT'S ALL A QUESTION OF WHAT YOU WANT

IT'S ALL A QUESTION OF WHAT YOU WANT

RHYTHM-MAKERS

COMPRESSION

Unlike type the written letter can be given great freedom in alignment and certain strokes, such as the tails of *R*, *K* and *Y*, can be extended for expressive effect, as shown above.

Pen-written capitals may be condensed to give taller letters in a given space, but *M* and *N* must not be allowed to become too heavy. Turning the pen further to an angle of 60 degrees produces a letter that has thinner verticals and is easier to compress. The resulting changes in stress and the thicker horizontals are reminiscent of rustic roman capitals of the fifth century.

COMPRESSION

Round forms predominate in this book script that evolved from capital letters in the fifth century and includes ascending and descending strokes. This typeface, similar to Hammer Uncial, (they were both designed by Victor Hammer) imitates writing produced with a horizontally held broad-edged pen and the typical forms with strong junctions between curves and verticals are made clear in the diagram below. An angled pen can also be used to write uncial letters, as shown in the alphabet below, to give a pronounced stress to the curves and a lightening of some junctions.

ABCDEFGH
IJKLMNOP
QRSTUW
XYZ

Typeface: American Uncial

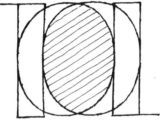

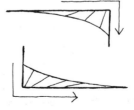

Serifs can be added to the beginnings of vertical strokes with an extra diagonal mark filling the space between the vertical and the lead-in hairline. For horizontal strokes the pen should be twisted as it travels from left to right, beginning or ending at 90 degrees depending on whether the serif begins or finishes the stroke.

Half-uncials

Like the uncial, the *half-uncial* letter is a transitional form and closely linked with the spread of Christianity and the writing of ecclesiastical manuscripts. Several minuscule letters such as *e, f, m* and *r* are already fully developed in these letters, while *g* is still in an intermediate form. The grandeur of uncial letters and the more fluid quality of half-uncials are seen in the two examples below, *Anglo-Saxon* using a more familiar form of *g*.

ab defgk
lmhrxy

THE RULE OF
ST·BENEDICT

Anglo·Saxon

Because of its strong associations with early Christian art and its archaic flavour uncial has few uses today, but its unusual and unconventional forms can be the basis for creative experiment. A title of compressed, closely grouped uncials, below, and a monoline design that mixes uncial with half-uncial letters, below right, illustrate two possible graphic approaches.

the
making of
letters

the
making
of
letters

22 Minuscules

The *minuscule* script of the ninth century, which evolved from earlier styles including uncials, later became the model for the first roman printing types in the fifteenth century. This twentieth-century example of a lowercase roman type is Bruce Rogers' Centaur. The basic structure and the broad-edged pen's simple stroke-making sequence in this minuscule script is shown in the diagram and alphabet below. Pen angle is 30 degrees and the main body of the letters is five pen widths high, with ascenders and descenders extending for approximately three-quarters of the body height. Double foot serifs can follow the styles described on page 18, and the angled serifs for some verticals are shown at the foot of this page.

abcdefghijk
lmnopqrst
uvwxyz

Typeface: Centaur

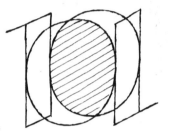

The Alphabet

Capital initial letters should be shorter than the height of ascending strokes and the treatment of serifs in both alphabets should be consistent.

As with other scripts already described the ratio of pen width to letter height can be varied considerably, as in the two examples shown right. Single serifs in both these examples give the lettering greater liveliness than in the formal rendering above.

Prospectus

twenty six

Arabic numerals first appeared in a European manuscript in the tenth century and are shown here in the non-ranging style that matches minuscule letters.

1234567890

The effect of compressing letters whose basic structure is circular has already been seen in this book (see pages 17, 19, 21) and here this gives the pattern of these minuscule forms a strong vertical bias with an increase in weight – a preview of the more angular styles to come.

Scriptorium

Blackletter

The complex group of Gothic scripts known as *blackletter* is commonly thought to be embodied in the kind of typeface shown here, Old English, but this is only one style, *textura*, amid several, of which three others, *fraktur*, *schwabacher* and *rotunda* will also be described in these pages. These scripts evolved during the period 1300–1500, developing gradually from the preceding minuscule letter to the most extremely compressed and angular form called textura. The first printing type, cast in Mainz in the mid-fifteenth century by Johann Gutenberg, was based on textura script. Although immensely powerful and decorative, compared with the simplicity and naturalness of uncial and minuscule scripts, blackletter characters are highly contrived, artificial and relatively illegible. In the English-speaking world blackletter can today appear anachronistic or medieval, but in German-speaking cultures it has survived in everyday use and their lettering is the richer for it.

It can be difficult to use blackletter in contemporary graphics – its medieval associations can be overwhelming – but if kept simple and free from elaborate detail these letters offer the designer a powerful alternative to roman scripts, and may be a basis for further experiment as shown on page 58. Capital letters for use with these scripts are shown on pages 26–27.

Typeface: Old English

In the four blackletter styles shown here the differences between each alphabet have been emphasised to an extent that is not always evident in historical examples. Serifs and decorative details have been severely curtailed for the sake of clarity, and the reader should find the stroke-making sequence in each alphabet easy to work out. Pen angle varies from 30 to 45 degrees and the 45 degree foot serif and the double serifs that may end some ascenders and descenders are shown right.

Textura

This style is almost devoid of curves, being made up mostly from short, straight strokes meeting at angles. It is a very narrow letter in which the blackness of the pen strokes emphasises the white spaces inside and between the letters. Ascenders and descenders are short – minimal line spacing increases the textural pattern – and may end in double serifs.

abcdefghijklmn
opqrstuvwxyz

Fraktur

The appearance of this script is less
angular than textura because of the
presence of some curved strokes and
the softer treatment of some details. In
contrast with the curves the straight
strokes meeting at angles look frac-
tured or broken – hence the name
fraktur.

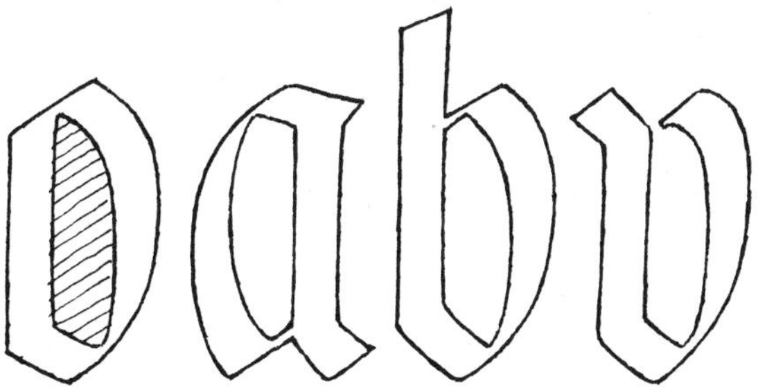

abcdefghijklmn
opqrstuvwxyz

Schwabacher

A predominance of curved strokes
makes this the least severe of these
blackletter styles. The pointed *o* and *e*
are very characteristic.

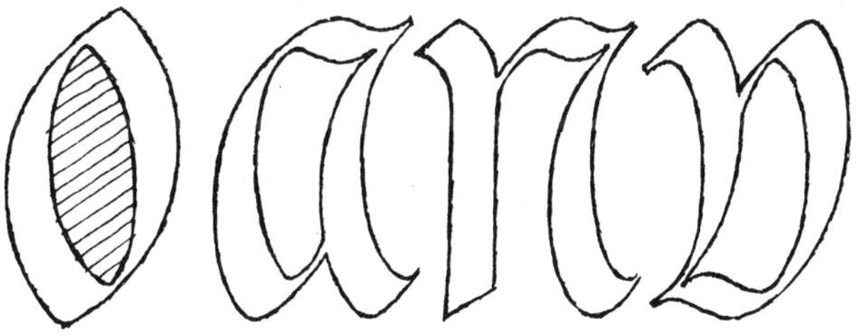

abcdefghijklmn
opqrstuvwxyz

Rotunda

This letter flourished in southern
Europe, especially in Italy and Spain.
As its name implies it is a rounder,
wider character than the other styles
depicted here, having more affinity
with minuscule letters (see page 22).
The two-storey *a* is similar.

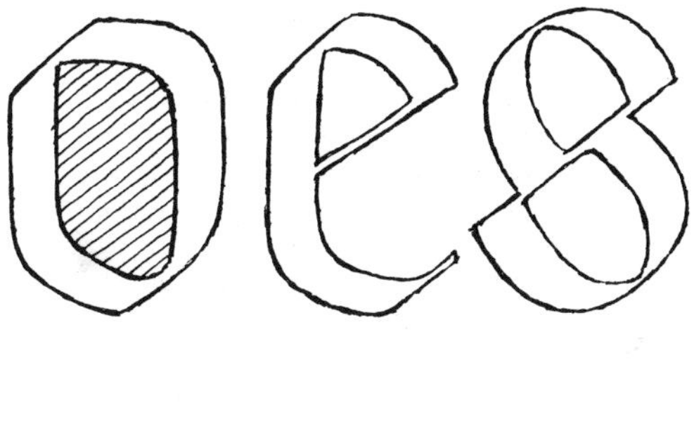

Capitals

Gothic capital letters used as initials
were often very complex and illegible,
so today simpler forms are better. The
early practice that based capitals on
uncial forms (see page 20) may be fol-
lowed, as shown in this alphabet (right)
which uses a 30 degree pen angle.
Below a variant using some typically
Gothic capitals that include many
curved strokes is shown, and ways in
which further embellishment may be
added with extra strokes are suggested
in the margins. The degree to which
the designer embellishes these capitals
is partly a matter of taste, but good
historical examples should be studied
too (see Bibliography, page 64).

ABCDEFG
HIJKLMM
NNOPQRS
TUVWXYZ

ABCDEFG
HIJKLMNO
PQRSTUV
WMXYYZ

ABCDEFG
HIJKLMN
OPQRSTU
VWXYZ

An alternative to uncial-based capitals is the pen-written roman capital alphabet shown left. There are distinctive junctions in some letters that provide a stylistic link with blackletter scripts, as does the angular *K*. A horizontal stroke across the top of *A* – as in the alphabet opposite – would add a further authentic touch.

Very simple, almost sanserif roman capitals, which contrast strongly with the calligraphic text style, can be very effective. The alphabet shown below, which uses a horizontal stroke on *J* and leaves the middle horizontal of *B* unconnected to match *P* and *R*, has been given extra strength by overlapping the pen strokes to make shapely wedge-shaped stroke endings. The pen angle must vary considerably to achieve this effect, which is shown in detail in the margins.

Changes in line, form and weight

Changes in line, form and weight

Changes in line, form and weigh

the Piano player

Blackletter has been much neglected in the graphic arts or used only in a narrow hackneyed way to suggest the middle ages or the antique. Some of the power, beauty and graphic potential of blackletter is evident in the examples on this and the opposite page.

Reducing the ratio between pen width and letter height results in a progressively blacker appearance to the groups of textura shown at the top of this page, the powerful pattern of the blackest example greatly reducing legibility — but high legibility is not always the purpose of lettering. The initial stands clear of the script to avoid disturbing the vertical pattern.

Increasing the height of textura letters gives them an even stronger vertical emphasis, as shown above. A double stroke initial provides a contrast of curves in this line of angular letters.

In the group on the right the straights and curves of fraktur are seen against plain bold capitals.

Myths & Sagas of Northern Europe

Vivaldi
Albinoni
Corelli

The Tenth Man

Decorative initial letters, and the curves of schwabacher lend a suitable musical flavour to the names of three baroque composers, above.

Below, rotunda letters are used in two sizes for this very apt quotation from George Bernard Shaw.

Fanfare

The golden rule

The examples above show three graphic treatments of written letters, including the use of outline drawing and a screen tint to reduce visual weight.

is that there are no golden rules

Italics

Narrow letters at a modest slope characterise the *italic* script of the fifteenth century on which the typeface Bembo is based. In its written form the pen angle is close to 35 degrees and the letters are slightly sloped at about 5 degrees, as shown in the diagram below, while the alphabet shows the stroke sequence as well as alternative characters and stroke endings. The compressed oval of the *o* is echoed in several letters and thin upswept diagonals and steeply angled serifs contribute to the cursive effect.

abcdefghijk
lmnopqrstu
vwxyz

Typeface: Bembo

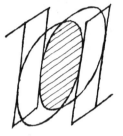

abcdefgghijkl
mnopqrstuvw
xyz·ypbdhk

Serifs may be made in a tight curve at start and finish of strokes, or given an acute sharpness (far right).

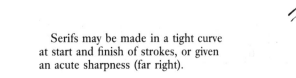

Initial capitals may be upright romans, kept quite short (right) or sloped to match the script (below) while the lower example uses a swash on the initial *B*. The three examples here also show different pen width to letter height ratios, and the word *Bibliophile* uses the alternative forms of ascender and descender shown on the previous page, varying the ascender heights to avoid monotony. Slight variations in letter slope will also avoid a monotonous regularity in italic, particularly where several lines of writing occur.

Fine &

Dandy

Alternative

Bibliophile

Ampersands are a space-saving and decorative device and several varieties may be used with italic scripts, choice depending on the kind of effect desired.

& & & & & & &

The already narrow forms of italic can be further compressed, steepening the thin diagonals (right) or lifting the pen to make a higher junction (far right). Very compressed letters look best with a minimum slope, and may even be upright.

The informality of handwriting with many letters joining is suggested in the cursive script below.

snap neo

The Chairman's secretary

32 Copperplate

This group of scripts, that flourished from 1600–1800, were written with flexible pens (see page 14) or engraved on copper printing plates. The typeface Youthline Script is one of many to imitate the style of *copperplate* writing, having a slope of 40 degrees. The basic forms of the style are shown in the diagram below, with an alphabet of unstressed letters and several characters written with the pressure variations that produce a thickening of some strokes and curves. Much practice is needed to maintain regularity of slope and rhythmical pen pressure. Guidelines and the letter slope indicated in pencil are essential, and it is also helpful to turn the paper away from the horizontal.

Typeface: Youthline Script (capitals opposite)

The pointed brush, which responds to the slightest pressure, is able to render a copperplate style in several weights and degrees of refinement, and may be used forcefully to produce bold and informal letters. The Mars 3000 pen makes lines of both delicacy and softness while remaining flexible enough to produce bold swelling lines under pressure.

*A B C D E F G H I
J K L M N O P Q R
S T U V W X Y Z*

Capital letters in the copperplate style are reserved for initials – like blackletter initials they are too complex to be used together – and are formed by similar writing movements and pressure variations as in the script. Historically they were often considerably taller than the script letter, as shown right, but today they may be shortened (below).

Penman

Penman

Some alternative serifs and stroke endings are shown right. The curved hairline serif is sometimes replaced by a plain horizontal cut-off, which may be slightly concave on the baseline to avoid a flat-footed appearance. A more natural sloped ending to the start and finish of downstrokes is shown far right, together with the typical endings that arise from ink build-up at the ends of fine curves. These are seen in the words below which, like most copperplate used in the graphic arts, have been drawn to simulate the script letter.

Birth and Education

While writing with the pointed brush employs similar manipulation of pressure as pen-written copperplate script, the visual results can be very different, as shown in *menu*, where the brush has been used at an angle to obtain the widest possible downstrokes and sharply angled endings.

As an exuberant extension to some letters the flourish has long been used to enhance writing, often attaining great intricacy of pattern, especially in the eighteenth and nineteenth centuries. The broad-edged pen flourishes (right) show a constant pen angle of about 30 degrees, while below are some typical *swash* letters including two examples (*h* and *d*) of contrived flourishes that seriously detract from the legibility of these letters. In the word below the swash on the middle *e* breaks the word in two – this character is best used at the end of a line. Lyn Gathercole's bookplate uses a long back-swept flourish to balance the lettering and fill the space beneath. In the sequence below right the unadorned word is progressively dressed up in flourishes, the final version's lower flourish extending from the capital because the other letters are not capable of downward extension. Whether this fifth state is better than the others is a matter of taste.

The flourishes (right) are not broad-edged pen based but derive from copperplate engraving practice, the lines swelling and thinning freely to suit the decorative effect. In the title below the surrounding flourishes, which do not connect with the words, have been drawn with the aid of French curves and a technical pen (see detail).

Flourishing is a difficult art to master, especially today when it can easily look anachronistic or like fancy dress. Restraint is normally the best policy. It is worth studying the work of the few contemporary masters, such as Reynolds Stone, Leo Wyatt (both engravers), Jean Larcher and Claude Mediavilla for examples of flourishing handled with assurance and taste.

Experimenting with non-calligraphic pens and brushes or even non-pens can produce exciting and unpredictable results.

Balsa wood

Soft and very absorbent strips of balsa wood make good pens for large writing but need to be dipped into the ink frequently. Cut the wood at an angle to suit your hand. The alphabet shown here is suitable for writing with balsa wood following the varying pen angle sequence shown in the diagram. This letter is reminiscent of Rudolf Koch's Neuland typeface.

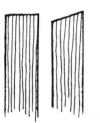

ABCDEFGHIJ
KLMNOPQRS
TUVWXYZ

The rapid ink loss and frequent re-loading of a balsa wood pen can lead to considerable variations in tone, especially when the ink is non-waterproof as in this example (right).

except

MAGNA CARTA

If the wood's edge is broken unevenly cruder letters result, as in the line above, while the group on the right shows that each letter *a* is different, depending on the amount of ink the wood retains.

Ruling pen

The draughtsman's ruling pen, with its screw adjustment to control line width, can produce writing of great vigour, as these examples show. Varying the angle of the pen controls ink flow; the shallower the angle the greater the flow. Speedy execution is necessary to prevent flooding. The German letterer Fritz Poppl was largely responsible for developing this technique.

Round brush

The freely formed letter shown here was swiftly written with a large soft round-ended brush held vertically over the paper, its shape first sketched several times in the air above the surface of the paper. Spontaneous letters made in this way have an accidental quality that is far removed from conventional broad-edged pen forms.

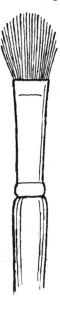

In this technique a pen of narrower width than the bold strokes is used to build up the letters progressively, as shown opposite and on page 27. Although slower than writing this drawing method gives great control over the forms, and if done with short strokes the overlap can give an attractively irregular edge. With larger letters white can be allowed to appear between strokes to further enliven the effect. Other possibilities include leaving white space between the pen strokes to make an outline letter, using pens of different widths and repeating strokes to achieve a multiple line image. This last effect can also be produced in single strokes with special multiple-edged pens.

JRR

freedom

MOS

prose ao

Graphic techniques

The following pages describe some of the methods by which the written letter can be modified or developed for graphic purposes.

Re-touching

It is usually necessary to strengthen serifs and hairlines when working for reproduction, principally to allow for the thinning effects of photo-reduction, and desirable to remove irregularities that may seem out of place in print. Re-touching with a technical pen and white gouache also extends the letterer's control over the forms, enabling him to get *exactly* what he wants. In the example shown here the original was written at a comfortable size and the initial added afterwards, then on an enlarged photocopy the junctions were strengthened and serifs given a crispness they lacked in the original. It is important not to over re-touch or the calligraphic character may be lost. Finally the lettering was reduced to its reproduction size. For further reduction all the letters were again strengthened so that they would not appear too thin in small sizes.

In the example below pen-drawn letters are the basis for the highly finished, visually edited characters of a typeface. The display of four names clearly shows that the discipline of type design has not removed the letter's calligraphic appearance.

Cut and paste

Because of the control that can be exercised when working for reproduction even the most apparently spontaneous line of writing can be faked to achieve the desired result. In the headline shown here several exploratory lines were first written to assess the general effect and particularly the style of the capital letters and the treatment of their horizontal strokes. The final version was assembled from several pieces of writing, the best parts of each cut out and pasted down to make up the complete headline. This can be retouched if necessary before a photocopy is made to obliterate all evidence of the sleight-of-hand that produced this apparently freely written line of script.

TO ME
scoot
EWE
camera
whistle

Enlargements

Using a photocopier that enlarges the image makes it simple to take a piece of writing made at a convenient size and enlarge it through several stages to achieve a dramatic increase in both size and power. If the original has a textured quality or a rough edge those features will be that much more expressive.

42

Calligraphy

Developing a script-based logotype

Careful visual editing and re-touching have improved the junctions and other details in this very informal continuous brush script. The original, shown far left, has been greatly enlarged on a photocopier and the editing done on that image. Most junctions have benefited from the insertion of more white space, the initial letter has been strengthened, the space between *p* and *h* (the only break in this word) has been increased slightly and the tail of *y* given a more emphatic termination.

Following this refining process an outline drawing was made of the enlarged image and on a photocopy of that the background filled in with a black marker to provide a reversed image. In the final reduction back to the original size the positive, outline and negative versions retain the informal vitality of the original writing with additional clarity – a further example of the extra control over letters afforded by sensitive re-touching.

Paper

The writing surface should provide enough resistance to the writing instrument to allow good pen control, but if rougher surfaces are used, such as watercolour paper, a degree of texture will result as depressions in the white paper show through the pen strokes. This effect can be increased if the pen is running dry, as shown in *Zulu*. The example below was written with a pointed fibre-tipped pen on blotting paper, while the highly absorbent surface of a paper towel which sucked most of the ink out of the brush on first impact produced the examples (lower right) giving a top heavy appearance to *North*. Exciting effects can be obtained when unusual writing materials lessen the designer's control over letterforms, and experiment can result in useful discoveries.

When the desert sun goes down

Resists

A resist prevents ink or paint adhering to the writing surface. In the example (left) the letters were written in rubber cement with a strip of balsa wood. When dry a coat of ink was applied and allowed to dry thoroughly before rubbing with an eraser to remove all the rubber cement revealing the white lettering. A crayon pencil provided the resist on a strongly textured paper (below).

Rubbings

Rubbings may be done with the side of a soft pencil point to pick up the paper's texture. In the example (above left) letters were cut from Canson paper (two layers glued together to give greater thickness) and mounted on card with the counter of *O* carefully repositioned. After the rubbing was completed traces of pencil on the letters were removed with white paint. The example left shows the effect achieved with raised letters cut from thick, coarse-surfaced paper. Here the rubbing picks up the background to provide further interest.

Masks

In this extension of the resist principal letters cut from paper (in this example those removed from the first rubbing described above) were fixed to card with rubber cement. Ink or paint may be sprayed on or, as in this case, stippled with a soft brush to cover both letters and background. When the paper letters were removed the resulting soft-edged forms were bolder than the original paper letters.

Stencils

A stencil allows a piece of writing to be repeated, perhaps to build up a pattern, and provides great scope in the use of colour. The natural breaks in pen-written letters make a good basis for stencil cutting, providing the necessary links that maintain the stencil's structure. The words in this example were first written with a broad-edged pen then a tracing was transferred to card and the stencil cut with a craft knife. Acrylic paint is an excellent medium for stencilling because its thick consistency prevents it from spreading under the stencil. Here it has been applied with a stiff stencil brush using vertical dabbing movements, but other kinds of brush can be tried to obtain different effects. The resulting letters have a pleasingly irregular edge, and the paint-spattered stencil provides a further image.

Multiple images

Repeating a word to build up a pattern is a graphic cliché, but livelier ideas are shown here with the repetition of a word in varying sizes (obtained with a photocopier) to make a visually expressive image, enhanced by stippling with white gouache. Below overlapping and repetition build up a dense but powerful design. This latter example, which employed pens of various widths, sacrifices legibility for expression and therefore belongs outside the usual area of day-to-day graphic communication.

The written letter's advantage over type lies in its flexibility, its liveliness and visual richness. These attributes can be used to great effect in monograms, logotypes and titles, with longer texts best left to type. Several examples are shown here and in the following pages.

Broad-edged pen

The illustrations on this page and pages 49 to 51 were made with broad-edged pens, the design opposite showing contrasts in style and weight with bold minuscules and light capitals, while even stronger contrast marks the *FG* monogram with bold, chunky letters – the result of much pen twisting – underlined by a line of small, light capitals. The initial *A* uses texture and open-ended double strokes, and the double *GG* design makes an impact by twisting the letters through 45 degrees to match the pen angle.

In this title (left) a large initial is used but the main effect is in the diagonals of the three *Y*s. The uncial *E* increases the number of round letters in this all capital design, and a discreet joining of *N* with *F* is not allowed to become intrusive. Set close together the lines make a strong but legible letter pattern.

Both *Fourteen* and *Centaur* use condensed capitals with irregular alignment. In the first example the curved letters are squared considerably to marry with the straight characters, the long, angled serifs and rough edges contributing to its graphic energy. *Centaur* uses light, curvy capitals in a sweeping linear pattern.

Pen-written characters can easily be overlapped to increase a design's homogeneity as shown above where contrast in size and weight add to the drama. The design's unity is increased by horizontal ligatures linking the light to the bold letters.

In this cover design (left) an informal script has been written on a slope, the usually inclined characters' now upright stance adds to the energy of the design and reversing the writing white out of a black ground increases impact considerably.

Stacking letters vertically is usually regarded as a bad practice but here where they are all symmetrical and the intention is to echo Chinese writing the effect is pleasing, with letters that have a brushy quality.

The monogram (below left) required several changes in pen angle to achieve its rather oriental flavour, and its softly tinted rendering is given a sharper definition by the irregularly drawn outline – another example of the value of contrast in even the simplest of designs.

In the title at the top of this page very compressed angular italic is aggressive and war-like. The vigorous rendering heightens this effect. Below, the ruled horizontal lines provide both a setting for and a contrast to a freely written script, while the white space inside *Review* flows between the characters and into the surrounding area giving an elegant, fluid quality. The thicker strokes add an apparent depth to this design.

In this title (left) capital letters of different heights make three almost equal length lines (if exactly equal the effect might have been too formal). The uncommon form of *Y*, swash *P* and open-bowled *R*s give this design its individuality.

The title below, whose rolling movement and stretched out appearance perhaps reflect the subject, was written quite lightly with the pen angled and twisted so that its contact with the rough paper varied from the full width to merely a corner of its edge.

In the line above a distinctive movement is created by giving uncial letters a cursive slope more usual in italic, the pen's angle varying from near horizontal to about 20 degrees. This is an example of a creative contemporary development of an historic letterform.

When combining letters into a monogram it is often enough to look for similarities that can be exploited, as in *av* where the choice of the sloped uncial *a* provides an almost reversed mirror image of *v*. Strong diagonals and the close-fitting background shape which emphasises the spaces in and around the letters make this a distinctive yet simple design.

Brush and pointed pen

The illustrations on this and the following two pages were done with a variety of brushes and pointed pens, the first three examples on this page with the same number 2 brush. In the title shown right considerable variations in finger pressure were required to achieve the strong contrast in the built-up strokes, the almost vertical letters having similarities to eighteenth-century typefaces such as Bodoni and Didot. To achieve the fine entry and exit strokes the brush was held upright, as was the case in the line of script below, a freely written version of copperplate. Some preliminary pencil sketching helped to guide the brush and resting the writing hand on the other hand facilitated the sweeping brush movements in this large-scale script. Re-touching produced the final polish.

Showing a greater slope than the examples above, this title (right) was also written with greater speed with most letters being connected. The brush was held as in everyday writing, with the pressure variations less marked than in the previous examples.

The aggressive design *aggro* was made on rough paper with a blunt stencil brush held upright and dipped frequently in black gouache. Notice how in such bold lettering the white spaces become positive shapes.

The great flexibility of the pointed brush is evident in this monogram, the stroke starting at the inner point and spiralling out with increasing pressure to produce the background shape that defines letter *C*. The original was made at approximately one-third of the size shown here.

Beast has a scratchy appearance that resulted from attacking the writing surface in quick jerky movements with a flexible pointed pen dipped in ink. This form of *a* is certainly uncommon in calligraphy.

The line above should be compared with the two-line title opposite. It has a similar informality but shows the effect of holding a brush at a lower angle to produce bolder, more loosely constructed letters – a gain in vitality at the expense of legibility.

The Mars Graphic 3000 pen was used with very slight pressure to make the lines of capitals in the title shown left. The deliberate thinness of the letters expresses the message.

The soft quality of *Z* was achieved with a chinese brush, the horizontals built up from several gentle strokes.

The top and bottom examples on this page were made with the same bullet-pointed marker, evidence that writing technique can have a greater influence on the result than the instrument used. The initials are further examples of the kind of spontaneous letter made with a rounded brush (see page 37). The originals were considerably larger and it is debatable whether the righthand character, with its sprinkling of ink spots, qualifies as calligraphy at all, but nonetheless it is a recognisable letter made directly on paper with brush and ink, a graphic mark with a particular aesthetic quality.

CREATIVE
RANDOM
SPONTANEOUS
FREEFORM

Diploma

Variety within convention

The examples on this page show that even within a convention (here a flourished copperplate to head a diploma) there is room to manoeuvre. Four varieties of broad-edged pen scripts, three without flourishes, are as suitable and perhaps more contemporary in feeling than the copperplate cliché above. Blackletter, of course, is still a usual form in some European countries, not confined to antique shops, Christmas cards and legal documents. An attractive alternative to printing is the embossed letter. Dampened paper pressed over a card pattern will produce raised letters, but for more than a few copies commercial die-stamping will be necessary.

Diploma

Diploma

Diploma

Diploma

Calligraphy and type

For calligraphic forms to work in a typographic setting it is essential to use contrast, either in size, style or rendering. Most conventional typefaces – oldface, modern (types with a vertical stress and fine serifs) and sanserif – will go with calligraphic letters providing that there is a contrast in size. But it would be a mistake to use an italic script, say, with a copperplate style type (see page 32) even with a size difference, because cursive scripts from different periods do not mix well. A freely written script form, perhaps with a textured appearance, will sit happily in a typographic environment much as a drawn illustration does, and the use of large, specially designed calligraphic initial letters has a long history and is still valid today, as shown below. The capitals here are the crisply engraved face from the early nineteenth century called Walbaum.

T m n
oldface n
n modern R
E sanserif
E n G o

A S LONG AS WE WORK WITH THE ARBITRARY SIGNS OF THE ALPHABET, WE SHALL BE DEPENDENT ON THE PAST

In the expressive design shown right a large calligraphic initial is also used with type, Hermann Zapf's Optima, an instance where the familiarity of the phrase overcomes the danger of illegibility that is often present when an initial letter is treated differently from the rest of the text.

LET THE GOOD TIMES ROLL

SCULPTURE ETCHING ENGRAVING TAPESTRY WEAVING *Kaleidoscope* PHOTOGRAPHY CERAMICS JEWELLERY PAINTING

Contrast is again at work in the design above, the horizontals of the lines of type capitals (lowercase would not work so well) are a foil to the dominant script letters. The graphic impact of this design is increased by allowing the flourishes to leave the rectangle and return.

Calligraphic letters may be combined with illustrations more agreeably than would type, as below where the two short names are staggered to provide a strong interlocking pattern above the portrait of Janet Baker in a poster design. The bold horizontal rule acts both as a separating device and as a contrast to the strong verticals of the portrait and the condensed title lettering.

Finally, calligraphy as a major feature in a page layout shows again the value of contrast, with freely written letters that dance over the narrow columns of type.

DONIZETTI Mary Stuart

The broad-edged pen, the principal instrument in the development of much of the Western alphabet, can still be used experimentally to design new letterforms, as described below.

A blackletter variant

The angular forms and broken curves of some blackletter scripts have been explored further in the design shown here. As the diagram explains many twists of the pen were involved in the script's development. Alternative versions of some characters were tried using the automatic pen (far right) and ink to make the trial letters shown below. A distinctive way of joining strokes was developed by using the corner of the pen's edge to make ink flow in a thin line to run into the adjacent stroke. The quotation written out to test this letter's pattern-making potential is by Imre Reiner.

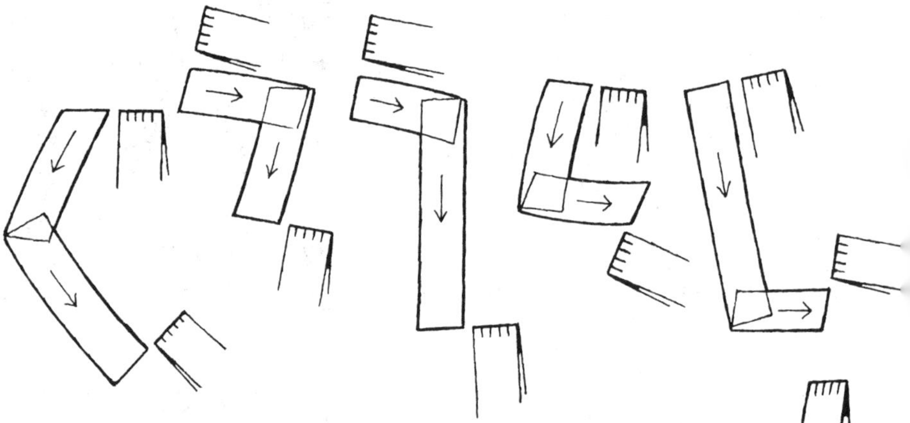

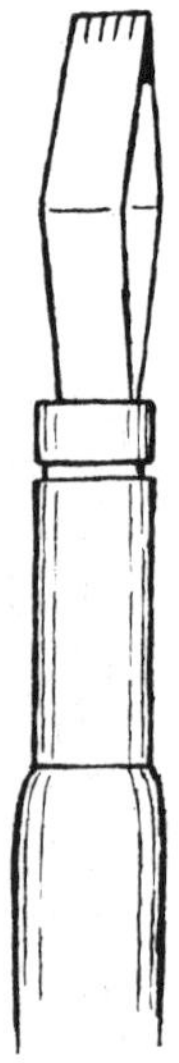

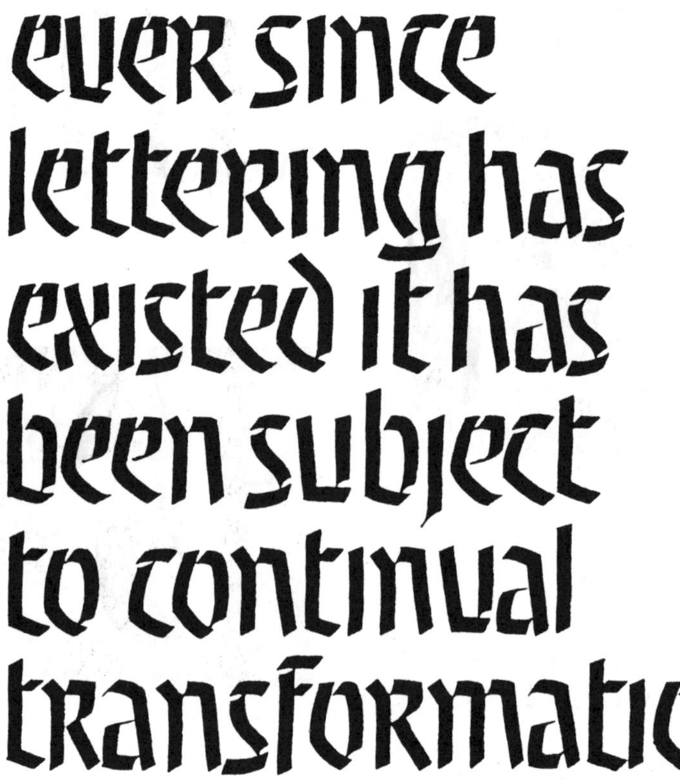

ever since lettering has existed it has been subject to continual transformation

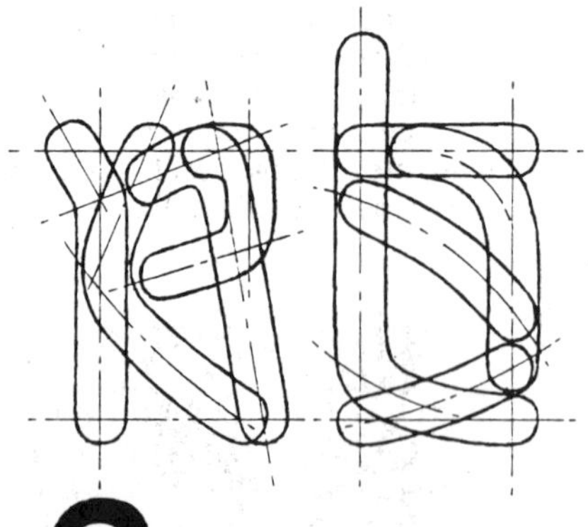

A further development is indicated here in these diagrams of a monoline version with rounded stroke terminations. Here the discoveries of an experiment in pen manipulation have been made into a formal system from which the logotype below has been designed.

bends

An unusual serif treatment

The usual, simple serif made by an edged pen when writing the verticals of capital letters is a lead in at the top left and a lead out at the bottom right. This gives a forward movement to the writing which Paul Standard dubbed 'the east-bound serif'. Conventionally the serifs that end horizontals in capitals point inwards (there are exceptions). By consciously reversing these usual serif formations a new rhythm can be given to the letters, as shown in the diagram where the conventional forms are drawn in outline. Several serifs now extend beyond the vertical limits of the letters and the wide junction in *V* has a strong backwards twist.

LET US THEN GO BACK TO THE SOURCES

This paste-up of a carefully drawn capital alphabet shows both how this innovation works on a smaller scale and the slightly flattened curves in usually round letters that help to maintain the new rhythm where serifs are absent. These letters are now essentially typographic in their orderliness and consistency of detail.

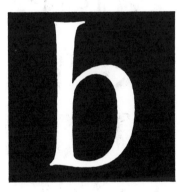

The same principles are shown above as applied to minuscule and italic letters. Junctions have been opened out in some instances to compensate for the space taken by the reversed serif. The quotations (left and right) are from the prolific American type designer Frederic W. Goudy.

Eccentricity of form from the hand of an artist who is a master of his subject may be pleasing

expressions of delight

The potential of brush and pen

In the combination of instrument, surface texture, hand and eye (also mind and heart) in writing letters the possibilities are endless, including the reworking of old forms and experiments in angle, slope and pressure to discover new ones. It is in this tension between eye and hand, as observed by the American teacher, Lloyd Reynolds, that fresh forms of writing develop, and we must remember that the eye may also be entranced by the hand's discoveries, leaving the mind to make a plea for legibility. A few directions are offered here in which the writer's respect for clarity has acted as a brake on wilder graphic invention, because he realises that in the graphic arts clarity of form is the normal priority.

On the opposite page the characters in the panel were made with various brushes, but the words below came from the same No. 2 brush, using different movements as indicated in the sketches. The reader will be aware by now of the role of pressure variations in such writing. In the last three designs the usual sequence of thick and thin strokes is not observed. The ascenders of *d* and *h* in *Slapdash* are kept thin to increase the liveliness of the pattern, and likewise in *Original* the usual stroke weight placing in *A* is reversed and the bowl and tail of *R* kept thin in *Extra*. There are no rules about this: the designer must decide what will work best in each case.

On this page of broad-edged pen writing the letters in the panel show several pen angles, weights and styles, while other possibilities are explored in the examples below. *Anger* was built up from several sharply made strokes of a narrow pen, the round elements becoming angular in the process. In the double stroke word below the pen's broad edge was turned onto its corners at intervals, resulting in irregular variations in the line and a slight loss of directional control. The white space enclosed by the pen strokes is very lively indeed. A very steep pen angle was used in *coteries*, a design with a strong horizontal emphasis. Usually in calligraphy the pen is pulled not pushed – the likelihood of it digging into the paper could cause ink to spatter – but with fibre-tipped pens or, as in this final example made with a balsa wood pen (see page 36), the unaccustomed pushing movements have provided changes in letterform and considerable expressive power.

Calligraphy into lettering

In this carefully pen-drawn version of
an italic-based letter calligraphy has
become lettering because the
immediacy of pen-written letters has
been replaced by the rendering of pre-
planned forms, albeit calligraphic in
spirit. As the diagram (right) shows, the
broad-edged pen was turned from near
horizontal to almost vertical to make
this letterform, which mixes flat serifs
with steeply arched thin strokes that
mostly do not connect with the main
strokes, achieving a degree of tension
between the horizontal and diagonal
movements. The two-stroke technique
(see pages 27 and 38) allowed the
waisting of each straight letter stroke to
be achieved easily, and the use of ink
with a resiliant steel nib rather than the
fibre-tipped pens that have featured in
this book helped control the finer lines.

Preliminary drawing established the
form of each letter in this alphabet
with the pen following roughly
sketched outlines. It is important to
stress that the drawing was done with
full understanding of what the pen
could do, so that the design which was
carefully planned by drawing was calligraphically conceived, with drawing
and writing interacting creatively. To
achieve an informal effect the letters
were drawn/written without horizontal
guidelines, and the usual lower serif of
f left off to improve the letter pattern
in this arrangement.

The italic alphabet lacks matching capital letters, but in this display they are set between contrasting torn paper capitals whose origins lie in typographic forms. A stencil effect (essential in the torn paper letters) unifies these very contrasting styles in which smooth contrasts with rough and bold contrasts with light. Three strands of contemporary lettering – the written, the drawn and the typographic – are brought together here symbolising their interdependence.

Postscript, bibliography and societies

While writing this book the author constantly had to remind himself that although the subject is calligraphy he is writing primarily for graphic designers, and because of this has had to simplify material and suggest short-cuts that may enrage conventional calligraphers. So the presentation is firmly orientated towards the graphic arts but the reader should not think that this is all there is to calligraphy. Far from it. These pages should be regarded as so many doors that if opened further will reveal to the interested reader even greater riches that may provide new ideas for graphic experiment, foster a desire to become a serious calligrapher (with all the study and practice entailed), or lead him to that area where calligraphy is treated as a fine art, as it was in ancient China and is now in the work of a few contemporary practitioners, especially in America.

The reader is recommended to study both practical and historical books on the subject, a few of which are listed below, and to seek out the work of the best calligraphers practising today, some already named in the text, especially those professionally engaged in the graphic arts, such as the following: Georgia Deaver, Tim Girvin, John Stevens and Julian Waters. These relatively young American designers work extensively in publicity and publishing, and produce pieces for exhibitions in which their creativity is given full rein. Also from America, where the current renaissance in calligraphy is most vigorous, comes the work of two very different men, Alan Blackman, a self-taught designer of very idiosyncratic letterforms who specialises in brush lettering, and Thomas Ingmire, the first American elected a Fellow of the Society of Scribes and Illuminators (see below) and an artist whose paintings integrate poetry, calligraphy and abstract expressionism.

In England the two dominant figures are Ann Hechle, an artist much concerned with the connection between language and form, and Donald Jackson, a consummate calligrapher as well as an inventive explorer of colour, form and texture in dramatic exhibition pieces. The German lettering tradition is particularly strong, its calligraphic roots never being severed, with the great teacher Rudolf Koch's influence still apparent in the work of men so different as Karlgeorg Hoefer (a master of brush scripts) and Hermann Zapf, whose calligraphic skill informs his many type designs, such as Palatino and Zapf Chancery. France has not produced many calligraphers of note, but Jean Larcher, an inventive designer of logotypes, is a vigorous practitioner

and promoter of the broad-edged pen through his books and teaching. Finally, in Estonia, the work of Villu Toots combines technical virtuosity with formal inventiveness, delighting and enthralling afficionados throughout the world, the language barrier being in this instance no barrier at all.

The more the reader studies good contemporary calligraphy the more he will appreciate both its roots in the past and its freedom, flexibility and liveliness, attributes that guarantee the vital element in handwritten letters and their place in the graphic arts.

Bibliography

Hermann Zapf: *Creative Calligraphy*, Hamburg 1985
This beautifully designed little book was brought out by the Rotring company in Germany in conjunction with their excellent Artpen range of pens. Zapf's text and examples are everything that one would expect from this supreme master of twentieth-century calligraphy. Available from Artpen suppliers or by mail order from John Neal, Bookseller, 1833 Spring Garden Street, Greensboro, NC 27403, USA.

Karlgeorg Hoefer: *Kalligraphie*, Düsseldorf 1986
A useful and compact introduction to pen and brush writing by a master practitioner. An English translation is included. Available from John Neal, Bookseller, by mail order (see above).

Susanne Haines: *The Calligrapher's Project Book*, London 1987
While mainly, as the title states, for calligraphers this book presents in more detail some of the techniques described in the present volume and will be useful to anyone interested in graphic developments of calligraphy.

Albert Kapr: *The Art of Lettering*, Munich, New York, London, Paris 1983
This large, beautifully printed volume with a scholarly text in English and several full-colour illustrations, traces the history of lettering and type, showing clearly the calligraphic development of early letter styles and the links between written and typographic letters.

The Calligrapher's Handbook, London 1985
Written by several experts in various aspects of the art this authoritative book is recommended to readers wishing to pursue calligraphy in some depth.

Modern Scribes and Lettering Artists I, London 1980;
Contemporary Calligraphy: Modern Scribes and Lettering Artists II, London 1986
International Calligraphy Today, London 1982
These collections make a useful introduction to the wide range of work being produced in Europe and America, much of it for graphic uses.

Gunnlaugur S.E. Briem: *Sixty Alphabets*, London 1986
An entertaining and informative collection of alphabets, together with their designer's comments, that shows how vital and varied today's lettering can be.

Calligraphy Review
This well-produced quarterly journal covers all aspects of calligraphy, including articles on historical scripts, the work of contemporary artists, reviews of books and exhibitions and some technical material. Excellent illustrations abound in this quality journal which is available in specialist shops or by subscription from Calligraphy Review, 2421 Wilcox Drive, Norman, OK 73069–3956, USA.

Societies

Once caught up in the pleasures and frustrations of calligraphy it can be a great benefit to join a calligraphic society. These organise meetings, exhibitions, lectures and classes, as well as in many cases producing journals. The main societies are listed below

Society of Scribes and Illuminators Founded in 1921 by students of Edward Johnston, the founder of much of contemporary calligraphy, this society is still thriving. Most serious calligraphers belong to it and to be elected to Fellowship is the most highly prized achievement in the calligraphers' world. It publishes an informative and lively journal called *The Scribe*. Membership enquiries to the Honorary Secretary, 54 Boileau Road, London SW13 9BL.

Friends of Calligraphy The main West Coast society in America, producing an occasional journal. Membership enquiries to PO BOX 5194, San Francisco, CA 94101, USA.

Society of Scribes A major East Coast society in America that organised the annual international calligraphic conference in 1986. Membership enquiries to PO BOX 933, New York, NY 10150, USA.

Colleagues of Calligraphy This important society in the mid-west of America organised the first international calligraphy conference, in 1981 and the fourth in 1984. They publish a regular newsletter. Membership enquiries to PO BOX 4024, St Paul, MN 55104–0024, USA.